OF EARTH

Poems 1964-1974

Douglas Worth

WILLIAM L. BAUHAN, PUBLISHER
DUBLIN, NEW HAMPSHIRE

COPYRIGHT © 1974 BY DOUGLAS WORTH
ALL RIGHTS RESERVED
LIBRARY OF CONGRESS CATALOG CARD NO. 74-83325
ISBN: 0-87233-036-2

FOR PERMISSION TO REPRINT SOME OF THESE
POEMS, THE AUTHOR WISHES TO THANK THE EDITORS
OF THE FOLLOWING: THE CENTENNIAL REVIEW, THE
COLORADO QUARTERLY, THE LAMP IN THE SPINE, THE LITTLE
REVIEW, THE LOGIC OF POETRY (MCGRAW-HILL),
MEADOWBROOK NEWS LETTER, THE NATION, NEW AMERICAN
POETRY (MCGRAW-HILL), THE NEW SALT CREEK READER,
NEW YORK POETRY, THE NOTRE DAME ENGLISH JOURNAL,
PROLOGUE, THE SPARROW MAGAZINE, TRIPTYCH,
TROUT POEMS, AND WEST END.
"SIDEWALK DUTY" © 1969 BY THE NEW YORK TIMES
COMPANY. REPRINTED BY PERMISSION.
"MAPLE" REPRINTED FROM PRAIRIE SCHOONER, COPY-
RIGHT © 1974 BY THE UNIVERSITY OF NEBRASKA PRESS.

COMPOSED AND PRINTED IN LINOTYPE GRANJON AT
THE CABINET PRESS, MILFORD, NEW HAMPSHIRE, U.S.A.

Karen

Contents

CUPID · 9

I · Love Sequence

EVE · 13
DAWN · 14
AFFAIR · 15
MARRIAGE · 16
SNAPSHOT · 17
FALL · 18
SOMEONE IS LEAVING · 19
DIVORCE · 20
MAPLE · 21
ASH · 22
ONAN · 23
DEATH OF THE PAST · 24
3/21 · 25
SPRING · 26
UNLIKELY PLACES · 27
WHEN YOU COME INTO A ROOM · 28
THE NEW · 29
MOMENT · 30
TOUCHING · 31
COMING · 32
SPRING NIGHT · 33
OTHER · 34
COCOONS AT THE WINDOW · 35
MY HANDS DURING YOUR ABSENCE · 36
GIFT · 37
PROPOSAL · 38

II · *Notes from an Unborn Father*

ANNOUNCEMENT · 41
PENNY BALLOON · 42
POEM FOR BROOKE/DADDY/DAD · 43
OUR BEING TOGETHER · 44
LOOKING AT HOUSES · 45
GROWING · 46
PSYCHOLOGY OF LEARNING · 47
AUBADE · 48
COLIN WORTH · 49
STAR · 50
EVOLVING · 51
BARRAGE · 52
FATHER AND SON · 53

III · *Widening Circles*

SIDEWALK DUTY · 59
GHETTO SUMMER SCHOOL · 60
EMPTY CLASSROOM · 61
THE WHISTLE · 62
PROFESSION · 63
TEACHER · 65
ICARUS · 66
JULIET · 67
WAR BRIDE · 68
MEDAL OF HONOR · 69
LETTER · 70
AFTER THE HOMECOMING · 71
ANNIVERSARY · 73
VEZELAY · 74
EXCAVATION · 75
POEM ON MY THIRTY-THIRD BIRTHDAY · 77

CUPID

An arrow has been driven into my heart.

*When I try to wrench it out
it curls like a young vine
feathers and leaves dissolving
in my hand.*

*The days pass
into years.
Inside me I can feel something
healed over
slowly
flowering.*

*This happens
again
and again.*

*Once
prying open my chest
I found a nest
of throbbing
tarnished pearls.*

*Sometimes, just walking along
a green wind shivers
the meadows of my blood;
the air grows so lush and varied
I can hardly breathe.*

I

Love Sequence

EVE

About her ripeness hangs
palpable, aching to bruise.

Too close you could not breathe
you would have to crush all distance

until you felt that stain
of sweetness flood your bones

drowning in which you would drift
forever, lost, blessed, dust.

DAWN

stillness

the grass

heavy

the tree

waiting

to sing

the bud

folded

aware

the air

too rich

for touch

AFFAIR

The table cleared
she brings in coffee
and to make the bringing special
a ginger jar.

Empty
even of fragrance
it holds up
under the lamp

a childlike pattern
of blue and red
flowers
which we enjoy, imagining

not a meadow, but maybe
a sideporch garden
on an afternoon
without wind.

Come from her hands
for my delight
it fills up slowly
from inside.

We look on
in silence, sipping
at what
we can't say.

MARRIAGE

We could see it coming
on the horizon
a brightening

that rose, flawless
pointing
toward noon.

Lying, our eyes
half closed
in the meadow

its radiance
was too great
to look upon.

Veering, it left
a reflection, shaving
by which thin light

even the closets
we were going to paper
with roses fade.

SNAPSHOT

My thumb's pressure
in the tack, still holding

it curls
like an exhausted leaf

all but the features, still smiling, lost
and they a bit
distorted, as if suffering
the tension of being
committed too long to a passing
season

the eyes especially, those quick
naked creatures, caught by the flash
at the edge of their dark lives
ache
to be gone.

FALL

leaf
after leaf

slip quietly
away

surfeited
burning

to turn off
the light

and pull the omnivorous darkness
over your head

SOMEONE IS LEAVING

Somewhere in the night
a wing falls from a shelf.

Making coffee I discover
a robin drowned in the sugarbowl.

DIVORCE

For years the bones of some animal
lay rotting, wedged
somewhere inside the wall
of your smile.

Now all that's gone.
The professionals, who can do anything
have cleaned up
in time for lunch.
A fine dust settles over everything.

Still swallowing loose threads
of blood, paper roses, scraps of fresh cement,
you feel the side of your face
coming back
as through a thinning mist
the pain like an angry sun
begins to spread.

MAPLE

as if
burning
old love letters

one could empty the heart
of its weight
of yellowed dreams

and sleep
bone clean
and waken green

ASH

Thin

seeds

shoulder

the wind.

ONAN

Virgin, pure
the flower's cup
scoured

you have violated
no one, risked
nothing
yourself.

You touch the face
drowning toothless
as leopards in Paradise

as you rise
sniff the sour light
seeping from the blind
inexorable
kingdoms of the world

start edging
back.

DEATH OF THE PAST

At home
more white stands out
in a room

a chair is scraped from the sun
a bowl brought out
then put away.

After a time
a stranger's clumsiness
the look of a day

invites us to believe
we have come far enough
alone, and to what end?

3/21

not yet
the paths
glazed slush

long grasses, heavy
as women turned
in sleep

the sun a hard
orange thought
on the horizon

Nothing sings above
the sound of water
gnawing chains

but an early
redwing hunched
in bare branches

making husky
overtures
to spring.

SPRING

season of breasts, of restive wakefulness

the lawns are raging

young trees, their heads blurred
with French and algebra
stretch out their limbs
in silky green explosions

all day the traffic lights
hang around on street corners
shamelessly winking
lascivious glass eyes

UNLIKELY PLACES

ambivalence
as a way
of life

Everybody showed up
for the party
but no one was there.

speech where only lips open
sailing the shallows
of each other's eyes

Here and there
a word, a glance
thrown out in unlikely places

claws through
layer on layer of darkness
to admit one barb of sun

shudders
cannot draw back
its root.

WHEN YOU COME INTO A ROOM

The season
does not change.

The flowers, leaning in vases
do not suddenly revive.

Yet, something
in the quality of light

shifting with the eyes' focus, heightening
to new acuteness

harmony
of air and object, motion and repose

becomes apparent
that was not

while you were in the hall
or on the stairs.

THE NEW

It breaks within, shivering
bone of the past
to a maze of troubled mirrors.

A stillness forms, a silence
of arrival.

At every hand
the hard glint
of a diamond

chastens our turning
away.

MOMENT

you stand wearing sunlight
around you
the room dissolving

TOUCHING

husks of defeat
snarled logics
of denial
drawn slowly
under

the body a wakening
field
of desire
each bud, leaf tip, swollen
light films every edge

COMING

the contours of self
give way

clouding

as river
enters river

SPRING NIGHT

A tangle, your face
is nearly lost.
My hand moves up and smooths it away.

So close, your eyes shatter
to a thousand shades
of green.

Are you all right?
Yes. You? Yes.
Get the light.

Things from the dark
come part-way back.
We lie close in the cool night air.

On the screen, something
crawling
a rind of moon.

OTHER

books you are reading

whole landscapes inside you
I may never cross

COCOONS AT THE WINDOW

All winter, ghostly
fists
of summer
they tapped the pane

crusted with a thick
glaze of snow
buried
a month ago

in our minds
another
promise that had not
borne fruit.

Tonight, floating
above the sill, the wings
still
tender with sleep begin

to stiffen, trembling
as when wind
shivers the skin
of a sail.

MY HANDS DURING YOUR ABSENCE

In company
they slip away
to sulk in my pockets
or mock my words
drawing aimless patterns
of smoke.

Here in the apartment
they drift
from object to object
unable to focus
their desire.
Nothing they touch
is at home.

GIFT

My hand held out two plums
both swollen with sweet juice
one half-a-mouthful bigger.
We had been walking long
uphill, through dust and stone.

It was the slightest flicker
your hand made toward the one
in settling on the smaller
that let me know your thirst

the scarcely-broken arc
between pleasure and pleasure
that left me with a gift
beyond all measure.

PROPOSAL

There is no measuring distance now.
We cross night's waters without maps.
The smoke-filmed window brightens, washed with gold.

Beyond the myth of harmony
your kiss, the thrust of your words
your work-roughed hands
move me, their differing energies.

Sunday, the roads blazing toward winter
we drank light
leaves like wine on the snow

returning, the bed in lamplight
always new
whose sheets we enter
as one hoists a sail.

II

Notes from an Unborn Father

ANNOUNCEMENT

Two nights ago
cradling packages
I dropped a fifth of Scotch
all over the driveway.

One picture shows a fish
with toes, another
an egg proceeding on course
through the left horn of a ram.

A poet, I'm supposed
to capture these things
and I try

but the images
nibble my fingers and scoot
the meanings swarm
off the page . . .

PENNY BALLOON

Two inches tall today
already stretching sleepy
miraculous fingers, toes
in your dark cradle, lined
with softest weaves of our love

even now, lulled in the warm
lap of your mother's blood
in your penny balloon you ride
beyond us, preoccupied
with all you must do to survive.

POEM FOR BROOKE/DADDY/DAD

You addressed your father as Father
complying with that strict male wish
for greetings, departures:
a faint peck on the lips—
like wolves, a kind of polite
throatbaring.

In high school, when I tried
lopping off Daddy to Dad
you went along.

Later, signing long family letters
from Africa, then Trinidad
full of the secret lives
of insects and birds
you had three labels to pick from
under Love.

Home, between marriages, for two days
I came down after a long, rough Christmas Eve
to find you alone
in the living room reading the funnies.
You rose as I came
wordlessly hugged you
kissed you on the mouth.

OUR BEING TOGETHER

These poems, written with you in mind
are also for me, your father
and Karen, Dad and Mother, Viki and Ellen
I could go on

our being together, each part
of the same thing, that we can't escape

and to say we must therefore try
to love one another
obscures the point—
we are one another
we must try not to turn
from ourselves.

LOOKING AT HOUSES

Who is it running
through my head
from the door to that bush?

the living room, as we enter, in half-light
familiar
the heavily polished
piano, listening

upstairs, the master
bedroom, small for us, slightly
awesome
the door to the attic
cracked open

on the screened porch, someone has left
a pitcher of melting
ice cubes, mint faintly
breathing

the back yard a dream
of sunlight
and there
peering out from the roses
a stranger's face
with my eyes

GROWING

roots. irrevocabilities. What are we doing
the rest of our lives?

over orange juice, the vision
that this is eternity

if there were a quiet box in the attic
labeled OUTGROWN FANTASIES—
there isn't, though I feel
increasingly, the awkwardness
of Bardot's cleavage, Blake's angels
at the dinner table

Tonight, again, we walk
past shadowy hulks of maples
hands laced, around the block

inside us the child becoming
part of the growing we've done
and have to do

the air full of whirling seeds, the moon
cradled, just there, in that fork.

PSYCHOLOGY OF LEARNING

Buried all afternoon in Hamachek's
Human Dynamics in Psychology and Education
I look up as Karen comes in
with three tomatoes from the garden.

Soaking my eyes, I sniff
their brilliant ripeness.

Christ! she has grown these
from that strip of dirt
by the garage.

Cleared, faintly luminous
I plunge back into
"The Deterioration in the Quality of Life Hypothesis."

A month from now
she'll walk in
and hand me you.

AUBADE

the shadow play
of leaves dappling
your thighs

your breasts still fountains
dreaming
of children

that globe where I trace
mazed rivers, virgin deltas
a new world

COLIN WORTH

as if
like Galileo, I'd just seen
something fundamental, new

changing nothing, everything
remarkably
itself

that tingling
sense of arrival
setting forth

STAR

Radiant Lady, Love, Karen, how far
since yesterday—now everything we are
washes, is washed by light from this new star.

Lifting him from your arms, cradling him so
I cannot tell and have no need to know
where his warmth ebbs, yours, mine, begins to flow.

EVOLVING

here on my lap, as on some shore
at foam's edge, moist with darkness
life, new life
evolving, dimly casting about
in air

love, like new mountains
heaved out of the earth
above us, jagged, uncompromised
by the slow sculpturing
that follows birth

slate eyes, still muted
as the dawn
already the brightening
mystery draws you
on

BARRAGE

the constant weight, building
exhaustion

at 5 a.m. thumbs, pins and needles
the feeling you've got his arms on
wrongside out

the point when the quivering buzzsaw of his rage
spewing frayed nerves, grates bone—
when song, when even mother's breast
is no solace, the light gone sour . . .

"I keep thinking this will all be over
in a few days
so I can get back
to my life."

at the cleaners, remarking
"Well, it's only for the next eighteen years."
the white-haired, smiling lady replying
"Don't kid yourself, Mr. Worth—my boy's
thirty-four next week."

FATHER AND SON

I

Well, Colin, here we are
father and son
alone for the next hour or so
your tiny hands weaving, me at my rhyme
together obscurely borne
on the opalescent, brightening, darkening flow
of circumstance and time.

This morning at six
when I'd changed the latest sopping load
and was tucking you back
into the semi-darkness of your room
planning another hour's sleep for you
so I could do some work,
I suddenly realized I was seeing you
more as some thing I owned
to be picked up, admired, cleaned, and put away
than as a person with a life of your own
and no way of telling,
someone who, given the choice, might well prefer
not to go back to bed
if instead he could watch his daddy making coffee
letting the milk boil over, feeding the cats,
or just lie and look at the frosted window panes
sketching silvery angels around the green wine bottles,
and then come and watch me writing poetry.

2

I remember another study,
the heavy, closed atmosphere, intensity
of adulthood—so intriguing, awesome to me;
long walks through the South Indian dawn,
all pearled about us, shimmering
sunbirds exploding from bush to bush,
coppersmiths in the high, molten leaves
hammering the new day . . .

so many things in this world
never wholly resolved—
growing, we tear ourselves
from dependence to independence,
from there to interdependence,
and it doesn't get any easier,
each stage ambivalent, incomplete
anxiety threading every bond of love—
and to say, as I did in another poem,
"We are one another
we must try not to turn
from ourselves,"
seems right to me still, and yet
we turn and turn
of earth, unable to bear for long
the cold, the radiance of the sun.

3

The light is just becoming,
Karen sleeping two rooms away,
Bach softly flowing on and on.
Again I try to shape words to my life,
groping, beginning, along with you
who lie here amid the clutter of books and plants,
the rich disorder that surrounds my craft,
taking it all in, fussing a bit
when I leave you too long, until I must leave these lines
which have no meaning to you yet, and come
put my hand on you, talk to you, fix the covers, and look . . .

little other, little one
of us,
everyday you grow
both more and less incredible to me—
how must I seem to you
my head still swimming above you? maybe, each day
a little less unborn, more your newborn father.

III

Widening Circles

SIDEWALK DUTY

Still half-asleep, a blur
of sound and light
the children mill about.

Their brightness wounds me—
I feel like an old man
my scarred hands brimmed with precious
seeds.

The bell scatters them
some to assume
a world created for their blossoming
some to hang back
like riches cast by the wind
on stony ground.

GHETTO SUMMER SCHOOL

They'd learn more playing stickball in the street.

Here their gnawed pencils scratch silence
while the teacher, for forty-point-one bucks a day
fingers his crewcut and his manual
through six weeks' planned assault
on ignorance.

Only the fan, from the antiseptic hall
muzzled, grinding its metal teeth
has anything worth writing down to say.

EMPTY CLASSROOM

only
here and there
turning away
from the others
a chair
flutters its wings

and
at the windows
a few rumors, dreams
whisper together
or lean their misty heads
against the glass

THE WHISTLE

Now it is autumn, scattering over the field
the children at football stop, face into the wind
wind clouding with leaves a moment
losing track of the ball, the goal undefended,
the teacher's whistle, the captain's cry of dismay
calling them back to the game's necessity.

If I were a boy again, I might pay no attention
to whistles and captains, when wind came up
and made a dark game of leaves,
but I turn my head
and blow the whistle, and blow it hard again
as if I could blow the leaves back into the trees.

PROFESSION

1

I teach
English at the Junior High Level
whatever that means

Robin, unfolding
leaf by leaf
Emily Dickinson's seared
luminous heart

2

2000 tons of bombs dropped yesterday
the Red River Delta
running blood
'to preserve America's honor
from stain'

'Kontum will be saved
even if that means
the city's total destruction.'

America, how can I stop you
from burying Vietnam
or your elected officials
from desecrating the language
day after day for savage ends?

A poet, I make
a living trying to teach
a handful of your children
something of that labor
toward clarity

which is no instant
recipe for action
but an attitude
demanding what is
ultimately, perhaps
unwarranted faith and courage
faced with the maze
the mystery
of the world.

3

Dianne's 'We know our world
of imaginary beauty
has failed us.'

Keith's 'There was nothing on TV
but I watched anyway.'

Sharon's *To President Nixon:*
'Sir, do you call cemeteries
peace?'

Julie's 'Will the pieces ever fit?
I think they've started
But how do I keep them together?
Tape?
Glue?
No, something stronger
Love.'

TEACHER

the page, sinewed
alive

How can I grade
this wing
wrestling my fingers?

ICARUS

Below him now in the distance
he saw the diminished figure
turn and come wheeling back

too late
the wings molted
as the young man

exulting, on his own
at last, began
the dizzying plunge.

JULIET

the girl still
dimly taking in
his sleeping
shoulders, chest, the dark mass
of her life

at the window the lark, the gathering
storm of light

WAR BRIDE

Clear nights, the massive
drone of planes—
curled on the mat, she hugs
her breasts, singing
over and over, something
about the shining
of new pots.

This morning a letter.
She gathers herself
to read, holds it
unopened:
writing this, he
was alive
his spit in the glue.

MEDAL OF HONOR

March April advancing
while the cherry trees
spattered the hills like shrapnel

for thirty days, gauze
a string of tags
my lips could find no meanings

long mornings
on some valleyside I grew
simple as leaves

watching the planes
through the branches
swarm like bees

LETTER

The window frames the harbor.

Resting my eyes, I watch the sails edge the horizon
too often to always see what is missing,
or lean and drift with the constellations.

Come soon. Come soon.

My hands, once so generous with love's gestures
are crazy spiders, raveling, unraveling

their laughter, their bodies
press me

what am I?
the haven you sail toward?
the hard queen?

AFTER THE HOMECOMING

kept going
by his dream of her
pining
or fed up, even, forgivably
unfaithful,
at any rate, a woman
toward whom he must strive
continually, against diminishing odds

seeing himself
as the hero, passing through, slaying
his quota of monsters, surviving
a goddess' arms, a trek
through the land of the dead

arriving, therefore
totally unprepared
for her strength
the impenetrable dream she had woven
of him as the tide-broken wanderer
herself the haven

what remained of the past
between them, that first night
rousing stiffly
to wag its tail once and die

after the homecoming horns had faded away
left facing each other
ceremoniously at the long table
like guests who have outstayed their stories

like ships drifting crippled
unable to meet
unable to release each other

he mooning down by the shore again
she slowly mounting
the smoothed stone steps to her window
the wreck of her loom

ANNIVERSARY

Even the cross
six feet from where she kneels

bleached scarecrow
in a barren field

seems to be urging her
away.

VEZELAY

Richard, lion heart
come
to lay your sword at Christ's feet

didn't you tremble
hesitate
here, at the last

judgment
where the slaughtered
lamb turns executioner?

EXCAVATION

always
here and there
in the rubble
among the fallen
wheels, helmets, shattered
stone limbs, heads

the delicate
flaming
of a leaf, a girl's sex
millenniums ago
still flickering
from the charred page

in porcelain, gesso, crazed
that apple blossom
milkiness
of a baby's temple

unwearying
flower of light

POEM ON MY THIRTY-THIRD BIRTHDAY

*Watching you
drift now*

*folded
into me*

*my cradling arm in the soft
flow of your hair*

beautiful

*the blood still blooming
fading
from your cheek*

I cannot sleep.

*a son
a house now, land
of our own*

*Living
in evil times
evil, as I imagine all times
must be evil, and good
beyond reckoning*

*what does it mean to be
'responsible
adults'?*

*my presents
waiting
in the living room*

seed packets, tools

*under the painful gloss
of perfect fruits and flowers
the fine mysterious dust*

*the shovel
leaning heavily
in the darkness
pointing
its blade to the earth*

Of Earth

*For Patricia Morin
May 17, 1975
Douglas Watt*